Your First
CHINCHILLA

CONTENTS

Photographs by:
Mark Truman
John Seamons

Front cover painting by:
D A Lish

t.f.h.
KINGDOM

©1999 by Kingdom Books PO9 5TL ENGLAND

INTRODUCTION

Acknowledgements
The author wishes to thank the following for their contributions:

Joanne Morrison   Model

Mark Truman and John Seamons   Photographers

Introduction

This book is for owners and prospective owners of chinchillas and is drawn from my observations of these animals over years of keeping them as pets.

The responsibility, dedication, dos and do nots of becoming a chinchilla owner, together with their continuing well-being, are all covered. I do not presume to answer any medical questions or provide diagnoses; only a visit to a local vet, one conversant with this exotic pet, can do this. I hope the contents aid owners and instill awareness of this endearing pet. This is NOT a textbook containing masses of technical 'jargon'. Certain important facts are repeated throughout the book.

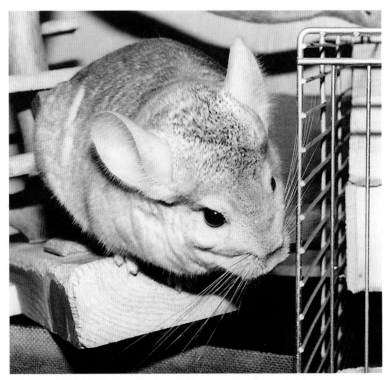

Ace Venturer - one of the author's chinchillas. Photo: Truman

Common Questions

Question: *Should I buy a chinchilla ?*

Answer: You have to give it as much thought as possible. A pet is not like a cherished piece of china, displayed, admired and placed in a position for all to view. An animal has to have lots of care and attention plus the correct diet. Chinchillas, unlike most rodents (such as gerbils, hamsters, mice, rats and guinea pigs), can live for a long time. Daily exercise is a must, to allow the animal to imitate what it would do in the wild.

Question: *Which sex should I choose ?*

Answer: The male of the species seems to be more extrovert and bonds better with humans. Females are more aloof, taking longer to bond.

Question: *What age should a chinchilla be when you buy it?*

Answer: Buying from a private source you can purchase one at four months old. This is an ideal age to enable you to train it. Some pet shops also sell them at four months old. I have seen them on sale at eight to ten weeks old. In my view this is too young for the babies (kittens) to leave the parental environment. Of course, older chinchillas also make good pets.

Question: *How about more than one ?*

Answer: Young chinchillas purchased at four months old will bond better with each other. At this age there is little of the dispute which can be experienced when introducing adults to each other. The latter is more time-consuming but not a problem to the dedicated chinchilla owner. Chinchillas are communal animals and love the company of their own kind. Of course this is advantageous if an owner is absent for most of the day and cannot allocate as much time to their pet(s).

Question: *Which colour should I choose ?*

Answer: This decision is up to the individual buyer. The common chinchilla has blue/grey fur. Colorisations are available but be aware that white, black velvet and brown velvets have a lethal factor when it comes to breeding. In my experience, white, black velvet and brown velvet females have a tendency to fight frequently, quite aggressively in fact. So, if you are contemplating these colour combinations, it would be advisable to house or cage them separately.

Question: *What kind of cage or housing should I buy?*

Answer: There are many cages available at pet outlets. When buying make sure the cage is roomy and has a number of floors. Single storey cage accommodation is a definite no-no. Caged chinchillas need a lot of exercise during their active period (which is usually when we are asleep). Of course, if you are an ardent do-it-yourself kind of person, tailor-made accommodation can be built. However, remember that the best kind of wood to use is non-treated pine, without knots if possible, as the resin from these can be bad for chinchillas. If using a manufactured cage, make sure your pets cannot hook their feet or other parts in the wire mesh. Its best to make all runs and contact areas wooded with untreated pine. You can always put smaller cages on top of each other, creating access into each.

Question: Will my pet get enough exercise within the accommodation?
Answer: Definitely not. Chinchillas are small but very active and intelligent animals who like exploring and athletic endeavours. So, in catering for this, nothing is better than letting your pet have the freedom of your accommodation UNDER YOUR SUPERVISION AT ALL TIMES. They are very amusing in their antics. Allowing them this freedom to be with you will also help you to bond with your chinchilla. If you want your pets to return to the cage, you can do this by using a favourite tit-bit to coax the animal back. I have personally trained all mine to return by word of mouth and a gentle tap with a stick on the floor. This takes a lot of time and patience but I have achieved it with both adults and kittens. The latter I exercise immediately on the day they are born; playing with the adults, they soon pick up their traits.

Question: I have had gerbils and hamsters; what difference, if any, will having a chinchilla entail?
Answer: Firstly, the greatest difference is age. Gerbils and hamsters are short-lived in comparison. Chinchillas can live to 18 years or more, so any prospective owners should take this into consideration if they do not want a pet which lives to a great age. So many pets are disregarded after the initial interest subsides. All creatures should live their entire lives with people dedicated to their welfare. Chinchillas are very intelligent, so they need lots of attention and challenges from human contact. Still classed as an 'exotic' animal, not so much is known about them compared to other 'rodentia' such as gerbils, hamsters, rats, guinea pigs and mice. One of their advantages is that having the densest fur of any animal in the world, fleas and lice cannot survive in it and you get very little smell from chinchillas.

Question: Do they breed like, say, rabbits ?
Answer: No. Gestation is around 111 days (nearly four months), so an active female can produce two litters in one year. Females up to the age of

seven or eight years have one, two or three kittens in their litters. They are born fully furred and with eyes open. Within seconds they are up and walking, investigating the environment surrounding them. This is when the lower part of the cage must be more secure to stop the kittens escaping. If they escape, fall to the floor and hide away, it can be very difficult to find them.

Joanne holding Cara. This female chinchilla bonds more easily with women.
Photo: Seamons

As soon as the kittens are born you can pick them up immediately. There is no reaction from Mum or Dad; on the contrary they do not mind at all. This is a paradox in these animals which are normally over-protective towards their offspring.

Chinchilla females will breed throughout their lives. The litter size increases in their later years, when each pregnancy may result in six to eight kittens. My experience with my oldest white female, who has been active since her purchase five years ago (she is now eight years old) has been the following sequence: twins, one, twins, one, triplets, one and twins. Triplets occurred; two were substantial and the third runtish, lasting only four days before it died. The two fit kittens were getting most of mother's milk and fighting off the runt. You could, in such circumstances, feed the third yourself, thus ensuring adequate milk intake. Naturally when a female produces a solitary offspring it is much larger and fitter than kittens in bigger litters. Do consider having the males castrated if you do not want more chinchillas.

Question: Where should the cage be positioned?
Answer: In a quiet, damp-free part of your house. Do make sure it is not within earshot of your sleeping quarters. Chinchillas (being nocturnal animals) will be very active while you are asleep. Contrary to some people's opinion, placing them in outside garages, shed or hutches is definitely not a good idea because the climatic changes will not suit them. They do not like water on their fur. Damp will cause a fungus to grow, leading to their ill-health and eventual death. Too much sun will make them overheat and may well cause cancer on the ears of light-coloured chinchillas.

Recently, on an animal tv programme, I saw a young couple with two chinchillas. In the cage, lying on its side, was a large glass sweet jar. A great home for chinchillas in a darkened room, but a death trap if the sun fell upon it. The inside of the jar, combined with the refractive rays of the sun, would make it a microwave and could easily cook the chinchillas. So always be careful. If you are unsure, seek professional advice.

The ideal situation for a chinchilla cage is a quiet, airy, room with constant temperature which is not used on a daily basis. Keep the curtains closed during the day, opening them late at night (last thing). Avoid placing the chinchilla in the bathroom or kitchen, because of the steam, and keep the cage away from radiators. Be sensible and choose a correct positional environment.

Question: Do chinchillas suffer bad health?
Answer: If the correct diet, exercise, accommodation and environment is provided, your pet will be happy and healthy with few health problems. However, if any problems do arise, a visit to your local vet is the answer.

Question: Will a chinchilla get along with my cat or dog?
Answer: Some friends of mine had a male chinchilla and two cats. Both cats used to sit in the cage along with the chinchillas! I have heard from other people with dogs and cats who acted similarly. Terrier breeds, some other hunting/aggressive breeds and feral cats will probably not be so friendly. Fortunately, chinchillas are very fast and have a certain degree of protection from their thick, dense fur. In the wild, attackers sometimes end up with just a mouthful of fur.

Eight year old white/silver female (Cara).
Photo: Truman

Chinchillas must be allowed to spend time outside their cage and suitable objects should be provided for their entertainment. Photo: Seamons

Question: Are chinchillas suitable as pets for little children?
Answer: No. A chinchilla's soft and luxuriant fur would interest small children, as does a soft toy. They would want to play with it and continually hold it, probably wrongly and to the detriment of the pet. A sensible 12-year old, under the supervision of an adult, could contemplate having a chinchilla as a pet but always remember that chinchillas are not as robust as rabbits, cats or dogs.

Question: What kind of person do you think would make a good owner ?
Answer: If a person wants a pet and cannot have a cat or dog, only a small pet, then the chinchilla(s) is the answer. For working people this animal is idea; being nocturnal it is asleep while the owner is at work and available for play and attention when the owner returns in the early evening. It is a pet for blue or white collar workers and people living in cities, towns or villages.

Question: How much will I have to pay for a chinchilla?
Answer: A common blue/grey will cost £30-£45. An ebony (all black) will cost £70-£100 because of its rarity and would probably have to be ordered from a supplier/breeder. Personally, I hope the high prices remain so, to discourage the novelty attraction and to place the breeding of these delightful pets into the hands of serious and responsible fanciers.

Question: How intelligent are chinchillas?

Answer: I believe American colleges and universities are carrying out maze
          tests on chinchillas. The initial results are that they believe them to
          be more intelligent than rats. My own experience and observation is
          that this intelligence is reserved and only available when they choose
          to use it. They talk to one another, mostly when playing and when
          they are euphoric. Time spent in the cage/house is similar to humans
          using the reference sections of libraries. Disputes are often
          patriarchal and matriarchal as they would be in the wild.

Question: Do you think they will become as popular as, say, rabbits ?

Answer: I sincerely hope not, so I hope they continue to be classed as exotic
          animals with a purchase price which reflects this.

Ace Venturer in lethargic mood. Photo: Truman

CHOOSING A CHINCHILLA

Choosing a Chinchilla

Chinchillas are shy, sensitive, nocturnal animals. Bearing this in mind, it would be advisable to see them during their playtime, which is late afternoon/early evening onwards. Therefore, if purchasing from a pet shop or outlet, late afternoon would be the best time to view and buy. Good chinchilla sources will order you your requirement if not available, particularly the more rare colorisations such as violet and ebony. I started with chinchillas bought from a pet shop and was well satisfied. However, I do think it is better to see chinchillas in full activity, either at a breeder or private owner's home, where the pets have freedom and can show off their athletic abilities and personalities. You should also be able to see the parents and other family members.

This female mosaic kitten only lived 3 days; she was one of triplets born to Cara. Only one survived. Photo: Truman

When choosing a chinchilla, look for a very bright round and glistening eye, full and luxuriant fur, and a bushy tail. If the animal is running about, look for good hind legs and that it uses both fully. Choose a pet that is responsive and not too introvert. If you are in close proximity, see if the prospective pet comes to you. This is an excellent sign and will inevitably lead to a very good pet.

Of course, chinchillas are communal animals and love their own family environment. They have very tight family ties and do not tolerate any strangers (other chinchillas) breaking up this set. I will cover this more in 'Behaviour'.

If a person wants only one pet, a male is recommended. They seem more affable and responsive to a human mate. However, it is my experience that chinchillas are happier with their own kind. After all, they may spend more time with a mate than with a human so, if possible, have two. A male and female combination will probably breed, so the prospective owner must take this into consideration. Personally, I find two of the opposite sex are delightful and, when babies arrive, it surpasses all. To see the parents dote on the little ones and to watch them growing up is an education in nature.

Your chosen pets should be aged at least three months old. This is the best time to introduce a combination of pets and to get them to accept each other. Buying and introducing adult pets to each other may be an horrendous situation, leading to fighting (see 'Behaviour').

The common chinchilla is grey. However there are many colorisations available such as beige, black, velvet, ebony, chocolate, white, white marble, chocolate/beige, violet and so on. The greys are usually the most reasonably priced; the dearest being ebony, the rarest colorisation. All colorisations derived from a white chinchilla born on an American farm in the 1920s. Never keep two blacks or two velvets together. For some genetic reason they cannot abide each other. If you are considering breeding, why not choose one grey and one colorisation? The babies from these combinations may have interesting fur colourings.

When you first touch a chinchilla it is like touching velvet marshmallow. Their fur is reputed to be the most dense of any animal in the world. They are South American (High Andes) Rodentia.

A prospective owner must also take into consideration the longevity of chinchillas. A healthy specimen can reach the age of 18. An American chinchilla has been reported to have lived to 22 years.

Finally, think hard about becoming an owner of a chinchilla. They are such endearing animals that they deserve a lasting, stable home, a home for life.

As a suggestion, a new owner choosing a pet for the first time should perhaps buy from an established, experienced chinchilla owner who can help enormously.

HOUSING

This three-tiered cage can house 3 adults.
Photo: Truman

Housing

You can buy what are termed 'chinchilla cages' from retail pet outlets. They are made of wire mesh with similar material shelving, a mesh bottom and a plastic 'drop tray' which can be removed for cleaning purposes. They are adequate but with one major reservation: the shelves should be immediately covered with wood, preferably untreated pine, cut to size and covering the entire area of the shelves. Similar attention should be paid to the bottom of the cage. Put in a dirt tray (a plastic one filled with coarse sawdust or wood chips). Attach wooden ladders to the sides and other internal areas. Perhaps a large apple branch could also be jammed in. The chinchillas will consume the bark, then the branch will remain useful for the continuing exercise of your pet. Other wooden items, such as shelves, can also be put into the cage. The more wooden items, the happier the chinchillas. Wooden items will have a relatively short lifespan, as chinchillas delight in destroying them, so do keep spares for replacement. When replacing, move things around within the cage, as chinchillas like changes and soon become aware of them. The idea behind completely refurbishing the cage with wood requisites is to avoid the possibility of chinchillas damaging themselves in the wire mesh.

A hut or tube (plastic, cardboard carpet tube or terracotta pipe) is a necessity for your pet's sleeping accommodation/hiding/safety place.

Chinchillas are very agile and acrobatic at night, bouncing and jumping all over their accommodation. This activity must be promoted to encourage a healthy and interesting lifestyle, so make sure that your chinchilla has plenty of toys or things to investigate in its cage.

Pet shops also sell cages in different sizes for housing pets. If you buy two of these, using the wire cage part only, put one on top of the other, making sure you cut an entrance on the top of the one below to provide access into the top cage, again using plenty of wooden shelves and ladders in both cages. Also put a small house in the top cage (plastic/cardboard tube or wood construction).

Owners may want to design and build a cage of their own. This is fine, but always make sure the wood is not poisonous, does not have resin knots and is untreated. Ideally, use pine or a fruit wood such as willow or hazelnut. The great advantage of self-construction is that the cage can be very large indeed to assist the happiness and well-being of the pet. I cannot over-emphasise that the housing/caging should be of the largest size possible and filled with activity objects to cater for both fitness and intelligence.

The single cage on the right is large enough for 2 adults. Note that all the houses, ladders and platforms are made from wood - the wires are never used for walking on.
Photo: Truman

L to r: Wooden ladder for access from cage to floor; wooden gym for exercising.
Photo: Seamons

Regarding the positioning of cages, it is imperative that they be placed above floor level, on a purchased stand or a table. If the latter, preferably select a table with metal tubular legs. Make sure the cage is never put into a damp or steamy room, so bathrooms and kitchens are strictly taboo. Similarly, avoid very hot rooms, radiators, open fires, gas fires and electric fires. When it is cold, supplement the heat by using a fan heater. When this is pointed in their direction you will soon notice that your chinchillas congregate near the front of the cage to sleep with the warm air blowing into their faces, looking so content. On hot summer days I draw the curtains in their room, ensuring semi-darkness, and cool the air using an electric fan. Again, they settle at the front of their cage and show much pleasure. Doors of cages/housing must be locked because chinchillas will open them and escape.

NEVER, NEVER put the cage/housing into a garden shed, garage or in the garden. Chinchillas belong with you in your environment. They require an even temperature, some fresh air, no draughts, no direct heat and no direct sunlight. Sunlight on light-coloured chinchillas will cause cancer on their fragile ears and other health problems. I sometimes think that I live with my chinchillas and not the other way round. I don't mind this because the pleasure they give me is unsurpassable.

Diet

Chinchillas have a very unusual dietary tract. You must always be aware of this and never jeopardise it. All animals will eat treats that humans give them, which can become habitual and detrimental to the pet, so keep to their proper diet and only give treats in small amounts.

Proprietary chinchilla pellets can be purchased from a pet shop or outlet. These are necessary as they contain all that a chinchilla requires, including calcium. Calcium is very important. One way of putting more calcium into a pet's diet is to buy a liquid form of calcium from a pet shop, outlet or chemist and add it to your chinchilla's water.

4 week old kitten enjoying a raisin. Photo: Truman

Make sure the feeding dish always has pellets available. Chinchillas will pick through them and toss out the ones they consider unpalatable and these become strewn all over the cage/housing. Once discarded they rarely go near them again. Feeding dishes must be positioned away from the floor of the cage/housing. One of my chinchillas lifts out a small terracotta dish and tosses it all over the cage, upending it first then throwing it about. This happens each day. However, using an alternative food dispenser makes sure the other chinchillas can still feed.

There is a new food available with grasses, raisins and pellets and so on. This is fine as an extra, but in small amounts. Their main diet should always be pellets (as previously mentioned) and hay. Hay and chinchillas are a funny mix; as soon as they have hay they immediately set about tearing the pile apart, throwing most of it away but eating what they consider to be the tasty bits. Again, I emphasise, there should always be hay in the cage.

When available, dandelion leaves (picked fresh and washed) are a delicious treat for them which they adore and speedily gulp down. Make sure they are picked away from traffic, ideally in your own back garden or a that of a friend, neighbour or relation. Always pick leaves near the centre of the plant's crown; these are newer leaves and so are younger and more tender. I soak mine in a bowl of salted water for ten minutes, then rinse them under the cold water tap. Place them in a glass of water and leave in a cool spot (to keep them fresh) until use.

Each morning all my chinchillas have a slice of apple. I've tried most varieties of apple but they seem to have a preference for 'Granny Smith'. I suppose it is extra juicy and crunchy, which they enjoy. In the evening they have a slice of orange or pear which female chinchillas seem to favour, the males seeming less interested. In my opinion fruit is good for them.

List of Extras
Rosebuds (washed)
Thistles (dried)
Apple
Plum
Raisin
Orange (not very often)
Pear
Kiwi Fruit
Liquorice (small amount about once a month)
Small pieces of toast crust

Chinchillas do not drink much water but make sure it is always available and fresh each day/evening. I boil tap water, let it cool and keep a supply of this. In the summer I keep this water in the fridge until use. Chinchillas in the wild get their water from dew on the High Andes flora.

Chinchillas love apple wood, hazel and willow branches. They eat the bark and bite off the wood in bits. The latter hones their teeth and is a must for pets in captivity. Again, DO NOT pick wood found near traffic. Wash (in salt water), scrub branches and hang out to dry. If the branches are quite large they can be jammed into the cage/housing. When they have finished eating and biting it, the wood will then be used for climbing on.

A salt block should be available in the cage along with a pumice stone for sharpening and reducing growth of their teeth.

Caring for your Chinchilla

Permanent containment in the cage is wrong. Although the chinchilla is small, it is very athletic and needs a large space to perform its activities. In the wild they are reputed to jump twenty to thirty feet and domestic chinchillas can still jump three to four feet. Their back legs and base of the tail are very strong; using their back legs they can propel themselves from the floor or jump sideways. Climbing is another favourite activity. Two or more chinchillas will chase each other round a room, retiring for a quick nap when exhausted.

A two and a half year old black velvet female - black velvet chinchillas should never be mated together. Photo: Truman

Baby chinchillas are delightful with their antics; on a floor they do a little bounce up in the air. You can see their pleasure and they like to tease the adults, sometimes jumping onto their backs to encourage them to play.

Outside the cage try to give them lots of toys and things to do, for instance you can provide them with carpet tubes, wood gyms, plastic tubes, terracotta pipes, plant pots, old leather shoes, leather belts, footballs, rugby balls and so on. The more entertaining the play area, the happier the chinchilla. Remember the more occupied the chinchilla, the more tired it will become and therefore it will sleep when returned to the cage/housing. The healthier and more contented they are, the longer the lifespan. Mine play seven days a week, enjoying the weekend when I clean their cage and let them play whilst doing

Joanne holding Big Baby, a two and a half year old female mosaic.

this chore. The sweeping brush, hand brushes and vacuum cleaner are great toys in their eyes!

As soon as my chinchillas give birth, that evening the baby/babies are put on the floor with the adults during playtime. Protected and taken care of by the adults, the baby/babies learn how to get about. One must at this stage be aware of them and take care not to step on them.

Time spent outside the cage MUST be supervised. As a gnawing animal, a chinchilla will try to chew practically everything, so be very careful of:
Electrical appliances
Cables
Toilets
Buckets/bowls of water (they drown very easily)
Wallpaper/coverings
Expensive antique furniture
Any furnishings
Gas/open/electric/fan fires
Floor coverings

Behaviour

The chinchilla may be described as shy, sensitive, aloof, endearing, dogmatic, cantankerous and amusing. It is a creature which takes a lot of confidence-building. Some chinchillas may be more aloof and it is a challenge to overcome this, taking immense time but with worthwhile results. When confidence is established you end up with a most endearing pet.

Respect is necessary, with a little strictness to counterbalance their dogmatism. So if you want them to do a certain thing, for example go back to their cage, repeat the words 'Up, up, up', tapping near the entrance to the caging/housing. Eventually they will do it and it will become habit. Always reward any achievement with either a treat or a lower voice with an endearing tone.

The male chinchilla seems to bond with humans to a greater degree. I would recommend buying a male if you can only keep one chinchilla. However, I do prefer more than one, especially when chinchillas are temporarily without human company. Their bonding together is to be admired and in the wild they are a great family animal. The adults nurture whatever progeny is around, attending to all their needs.

Within groups of chinchillas there is much debate to establish patriarch and matriarch status. Normally the skirmishes are light and do not cause too much anxiety to owners. However, if serious fighting occurs it would be best to separate the culprits.

Chinchillas look and feel very cuddly but are independent and only become affable when they want to. All my chinchillas have their own individual personality. Behaviour patterns differ depending on grouping. Naturally with one pet these patterns are not so obvious. If you have two males and a female, when adulthood has been reached by all three and the female comes into season, the two males will fight for dominance and the victor will pair for life with the female if they remain together. However circumstances may change, through death of the female or perhaps with the introduction of a new female. Again, the dominant male will mate with this new female.

Minding other people's pet chinchillas can be a trial. I recently had one of my chinchillas back whilst the new owners went on holiday. These owners had had the male chinchilla for three months. I was under the impression that, since it was the son of my oldest pair of chinchillas, all would be well. However this was not the case. The father fiercely attacked this chinchilla, so I had to telephone the owners to come and collect it. During this period of absence the young chinchilla had acquired a different smell and was perceived by the others as infiltrating their group, which is why the old male attacked it. Chinchillas become very protective of the group.

If a person already has an adult chinchilla and is considering buying another, this can be achieved. If your chinchilla is an adult male then, ideally, you have a choice of either a male or female baby or an adult female.

If you wish to buy another adult male and are prepared to be persistent, two adult males will eventually bond with each other. They must be kept apart in the beginning, so put them into separate cages to start with, side by side but not so close that they can bite each other. Keep to this arrangement for about two weeks and then have another fortnight of allowing them to run and play together on the floor. Initial skirmishes will not be too serious. Then try them together in the same cage. With this set-up never, never introduce an adult female at a later date because this will inevitably lead to fights between the males.

If you have numerous adult females with one adult male, baby chinchillas will be accepted by both sexes. However problems will arise when babies reach adulthood. This is something that should be considered if you breed and decide to keep some of the offspring.

Never mate two black velvet chichillas together; genetically they are incompatible. Similarly, two white or two brown velvets will produce a lethal factor in their offspring.

Within a group, chinchilla behaviour is often influenced by what the other members of the group are doing. Hence you will often see them huddled together, asleep or resting. At other times their individuality is apparent when they go into isolated parts of the cage/house to be on their own. In this case, if one goes near another you will hear argumentative noises, followed by short and sharp bites. When really annoyed, chinchillas use their ultimate weapon; standing erect a jerk of their pelvic region is followed by a jet of urine which is aimed at the offender - and their aim is very accurate! They try to squirt this liquid into the offender's eye. When successful it causes irritation which may last a couple of days. The stream of urine can be projected three to four feet.

Chinchillas make numerous noises ranging from very low to the loudest trumpet sound. The very low noise is what they use when playing and it is their way of talking to one another. When there is a small baby (kitten) playing, the adults keep constant track of the baby using this mode of expression.

The trumpet noise is the warning sound. Sometimes when one chinchilla makes this noise the others rapidly disappear into hiding. In the wild one of their predators is the condor (which has a three metre wingspan) so this trumpet warning sound is necessary for survival.

Finally there is the arguing/fighting noise and also a mating noise. In all, chinchillas make four or five separate noises/sounds.

Chinchillas are not pets that like to be hugged and caressed for a long time. The longest I have managed is ten minutes in my arms. They do like a tickle behind the ears and under the front feet on the upper chest, reciprocating with a rapid front-foot rub on your finger.

If you lie down on the floor and remain perfectly still, after a while chinchillas will run all over your body, pruning your eyebrows, lashes, nasal and ear hairs (if you have them) sitting on your head and maybe trimming your hair.

Chichillas are inquisitive and therefore must be supervised when outside their cage. Here, a 4 week old kitten has found a piece of string. Photo: Truman

They love stockinged feet, first nibbling socks or stockings, then sitting there for a while. This does not happen instantaneously; one has to lie on the floor a few times before chinchilla confidence is achieved. Staying still is the art for the human, any slight movement and the animals flee. Having three chinchillas on your face is difficult to describe; their fur is like soft velvet and, naturally, it tickles but you have to restrain yourself from scratching if you want them to remain.

Inquisitiveness is their byword, liking to get in everywhere they can. You must guard against this for the safety of your pet.

23

Handling Your Chinchilla

If possible, start with a young animal using lots of touching, palming the pet continuously, speaking to it in a soft voice. Keep saying its name and eventually it will react. Tickle under the chin and rub its upper chest, just under the front feet and behind the ears.

Picking up a chinchilla from the ground is a challenge in itself for they are very fast. Your response must be very, very quick; grab it by the base of the tail which is a muscular and strong area of a chinchilla. Once you have done this the best handling position is one hand under its head, the other supporting the chest area. Never grab the body of your pet whether it is in its cage or on the ground because this will hurt the animal and possibly do damage.

An adult chinchilla only weighs 18-30 ounces, not what you call a robust pet. Catching a chinchilla by the end of its tail will make the animal cry out and you will not only distress it but also end up pulling out some of its tail hairs.

With older chinchillas, handling from the start will take more time.

An adult chinchilla wil take longer to tame than a kitten would.

Confidence and trust have to be achieved first. A good time to build on this is when the animal is caged. Open the door and put both hands inside, palms upward. Let the animal sniff them; try not to make any sudden movement with your hands or body. After a time the chinchilla will come and sit in your palms, settling momentarily. Repeating this process each day, the settling time will increase. Eventually the chinchilla will venture further, onto your forearms. The ultimate (which will come) will be to lie on your back on the floor and the chinchilla will run all over your body. At all times keep perfectly still, even down to the blink of an eyelid or a sneeze.

Time is the great factor in handling; the more time spent, combined with patience, the more likely you are to achieve your aims.

Finally, to create an extrovert personality and facilitate training, it would be advisable to start with a very young chinchilla.

Out of the cage and ready to go.....

Domestic chinchillas can jump three to four feet high.

BREEDING

Breeding

A pregnant female has a gestation period of 111 days and females give birth to one, two or three kittens.

A female will continue breeding until her year of death which could be aged 18 years old. In her later years a brood could be five or six in number.

When a female gives birth she needs no help from a human and it's best to keep her quietly on her own. She will give birth in the bottom of the cage on the bedding (use wood chippings). The babies (kittens) are born fully furred and with eyes wide open. They are on their feet in seconds and ready to climb and run about. You can pick them up immediately they are born, mother does not mind whatsoever, unlike some other animals.

The following story is told from my own experience. At 1.50am on 25 October 1997 a baby chinchilla died. I did my best to revive him by blowing

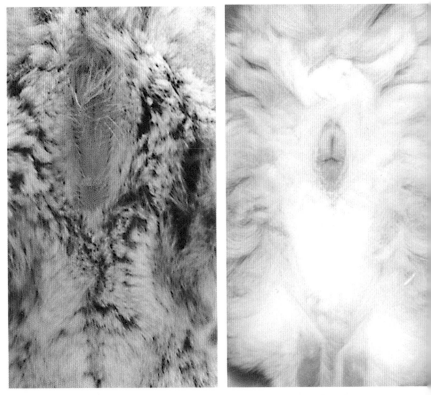

Sexing: male chinchilla on the left, female on the right.
Photos: Seamons

gently into his mouth and rubbing his breast to stimulate the heart, but I could see his life disappearing. There seemed no pain and little suffering, just a gentle rest, a couple of quiet, almost inaudible squeaks, and a four day old life expired. I felt so useless and frustrated that I could not perform a miracle, having planned earlier that I would keep this baby, knowing it would be infirm for its entire life, whatever that may have been.

This baby chinchilla was male and white marble, extremely thin, frame slightly deformed, noticeable blood from rear passage and around the ears. During the four days of its life the other two (triplets had been born) had visibly grown whereas this one had not. However, of the three, this male (incidentally born last, an hour after the others) was the most adventurous, being the first to get out of the cage and to run around the floor. He did this on three occasions until I boarded up the lower parts of the cage so that he could not escape again.

Pet death, in my opinion, is hard to accept however close you are to nature and her ways. Regarding the death of offspring, sometimes females give birth to stillborn kittens. I have noticed that it is usually when just one baby/kitten is born and is very large compared with those in multiple births. Perhaps this is the reason, the size of the baby/kitten causing stress and inevitable death.

On the subject of stillborn, early deaths, miscarriages and adult deaths of chinchillas, I have seen chinchillas, such as mothers, fathers and others that may be sharing cages, mourning. This is not a scientific fact but based on my own observations. Another noticeable fact is that immediately after a death the other chinchillas seem to be less athletic and become temporarily lethargic.

Returning to the subject of breeding, if an owner has to feed a newborn kitten the nearest to chinchilla milk is a mix of camomile tea and evaporated milk. The mix is two parts camomile tea, one part evaporated initially. Later, if required, lessen the camomile and increase the milk, but only by a little. The tea part is more important. Feed this using an eye-dropper or a glass pipette. The eye-dropper may be obtained from a chemist. Do not use a rubber teat as the baby will soon bite it. Be very careful administering in the first instance, making sure no milk goes down the nasal passage which would lead to suffocation and death. The chinchilla baby will soon take to the artificial feeding. If not, perhaps you could use a surrogate mother. Consult a vet about this to find out which alternative pet would serve this purpose.

Lack of milk in female chinchillas is common, mostly due to poor diet. I give my chinchillas dandelion leaves and fruit (as specified in 'Diet') and I am sure this helps with milk production.

Finally, babies seem to be able to manage solid food and to drink water. I have seen them do this within two weeks of birth. Babies (kittens) should remain with their parents until they are three months old before going to their new homes.

HEALTH ISSUES

Health Issues

An explanation of these follows, excluding medical disorders in which case a vet should be consulted.

Bathing and Grooming

Chinchillas in the wild live in rock crevices in the High Andes where there is little water. They keep clean by bathing in volcanic dust. It is comical to watch them bathing, especially when more than one chinchilla is involved. I have the dust bath available outside the cage at all times, sieving it each morning and replacing with new dust twice a week. A tip is to add a teaspoon of baby talcum powder to the dust. This makes a white or light coloured chinchilla's coat look cleaner. White fur does show up yellow urine staining around the bottom. I normally wash this area gently with tepid water. If you do this make sure you dry the area thoroughly, chinchillas do not like water or any liquid on their bodies.

My dust bath is kept on the floor in a tray 9" x 12", placed in a deeper and larger 15" x 24" tray (actually the plastic base of an unused cage). This helps to retain the dust because during use the animals twist, turn and roll, flicking dust in all directions, enjoying every moment, as you will whilst watching. I have heard of some owners who put a bath tray in the cage. I am against this as the flying dust may penetrate the food and water supplies.

Remember, chinchillas DO like an audience when bathing. With one of my chinchillas all I have to say is 'Bath' and he immediately goes in, does a few roll-overs then looks up. I say 'Bath' again and he reciprocates with another show. I do believe he would carry on doing this for a very long time.

Chinchillas are self-grooming. I have not often seen adults grooming one another, unlike some other group animals. However when kittens are around, the parents groom them profusely until they reach the age of five weeks or so.

If you have a very young chinchilla I recommend that you start combing out its fur using a nit comb from a chemist. This has very fine teeth and is ideal for a chinchilla's dense fur. Try to get a metal one and comb on a regular basis. It will also aid in handling your pet and cementing the bond between you and your chinchilla.

If showing your pet, a chinchilla should live on its own for the best coat so that its fur is not bitten by others. However, the animal must be absolutely content with this situation or it may start fur biting.

Castration

If the owner has two pets of the opposite sex living together, after a while he/she might consider having their male chinchilla castrated. Females are not as prolific breeders as, say, rats, gerbils or hamsters. However, chinchillas not being so popular, an owner may experience difficulty in finding homes for their baby chinchillas when they reach three months old. One has to take into account as well that these animals reach great ages and the female may produce offspring until she dies. Numerous people have told me that they have had their pet successfully castrated, the male being the easier option. Operating on the female is more complicated and involved. Alternatively, to retain both pets without breeding, it is necessary to house them separately.

Eye Irritation/Infection

A healthy eye should be large, open and glistening. If a chinchilla constantly suffers from watery eyes, a visit to the vet is necessary. Do mention to the vet that you would prefer eye drops if possible. The reasons for this are twofold:

(i) They are easier to administer. If competent, one can manage it alone. The correct way to hold a chinchilla when giving eye drops is to bring its ears together (gently please) with your thumb and forefinger, enabling you to get the chinchilla's cheek and head in the correct position for placing the eye drops.

(ii) The eye solution is contained within the eye region and disperses very satisfactorily.

Creams are messy, more difficult to administer and some of the cream inevitably gets on the hair around the chinchilla's eye and down to the cheek. If the chinchilla tries to get rid of it in the dust bath or by rubbing its eyes in anything available, this may cause further problems. It takes two people to administer cream; one to hold the animal, the other to put the cream in. The latter needs a very steady hand or the cream will miss the target or, even worse, you may damage the eye with the nozzle of the tube.

Fur Biting

In lone adults the cause is often boredom. This is because the animal may be caged in a single storey with nothing to do, together with no exercise, no toys and absolutely nothing to amuse them. Picture yourself in your pet's environment - would you be satisfied? I advocate that my pets have the most pleasurable life I am able to give them. It is a good doctrine to abide by. Back to the subject. After a time the fur will look very dowdy with pieces missing where the chinchilla has bitten. Its personality will be affected, with a miserable outlook and maybe cowering, not a cheerful chappy or chappess. Lack of human companionship will exacerbate the problem.

The answer is to provide your chinchilla with roomy accommodation, lots of outside play and plenty of human contact. They will also appreciate a variety of playthings in the cage/housing with lots of climbing equipment. That will put a smile back on their faces.

Within chinchilla groups, spasmodic fur biting is apparent but will not last for long. Fighting fur is normally pulled out, not bitten off. Fur and whisker biting is also prevalent when newborn babies (kittens) are with their parents. The mother is usually the one who suffers but this will gradually cease as the

Three day old kitten in a wine glass. Photo: Truman

baby grows up. My eldest female, Cara, when not with offspring has a most wonderful set of whiskers. They are very long and white and she is so proud of them, grooming them all the time. Chinchillas look like Chinese Mandarins when they do this and it is lovely to watch.

Lack of hay in the diet can also be a cause of fur biting. I suppose they consider fur to be an alternative form of roughage, so make sure that hay is available at all times.

Veterinary Costs
As yet I do not think you can get pet insurance for chinchillas. Perhaps if their popularity increases it may become available. Personally I have my own pet bank account for these costs, as well as for buying new cages and any other larger expenses incurred, thus financially catering for my pets. This would include taking care of their future if I were to die first.

THE DO NOTS

The Do Nots

NEVER leave any open containers holding liquid such as water, wallpaper paste, bleach, washing up water bowls, mopping pails or buckets, near chinchillas. Liquid on a chinchilla's fur will cause it to sink and drown.

NEVER leave your toilet open, keep the lid down at all times. Remind family and friends to make sure the chinchilla is safely out of the way before using it.

NEVER bath your chinchilla in water unless directed by a veterinary surgeon (for example when using anti-bacterial baths).

NEVER feed your pet fatty foodstuffs such as crisps, biscuits (human varieties), buttered toast, bacon, cakes, bread, sweets, cornflakes and so on.

NEVER feed lettuce or any other vegetable and NEVER offer any liquid other than water.

NEVER leave any electrical appliances connected when chinchillas are about. Turn off all appliances at the mains and remove the plug.

NEVER leave your chinchilla to roam freely about your premises without your being there in attendance.

NEVER house/cage your pet in an exterior hutch, garage or shed. The dampness will cause a fungus and will eventually kill your pet. (A chinchilla's housing requirement is dry accommodation with a constant temperature).

NEVER let your chinchilla out in the garden to roam. It will disappear quite quickly and you will lose your pet.

NEVER pick up your chinchilla by squeezing it. Always pick it up correctly by the base of the tail, the other hand gently supporting its chest.

NEVER grab a chinchilla by the end of the tail as all you will get is a screech and some tail hairs in your hand.

NEVER put your pets in direct sunlight, especially white, beige or any other light-coloured chinchillas, because they could get cancer.

NEVER leave the house/cage in very hot conditions. (An electric fan is excellent in hot temperatures, make sure it is placed it out of the animal's reach). Alternatively, in very cold conditions, an electric fan heater is a great aid.

NEVER put your pet in a busy, sunny room during the day (your pet's sleeping time). A quiet, airy and darkened room (curtains drawn) is the answer. Remember, a little noise will create an immediate response in your sensitive chinchilla and WILL frighten it.

NEVER put your chinchillas near open windows. If they escape from their cage, get out of a window which is high up and fall, this WILL kill them.

NEVER introduce new pets instantaneously without supervision. They will probably fight immediately and do irreparable damage to one another.

NEVER put other pets into your chinchilla's cage unless you are certain that they will bond and NEVER ever put your pet with snakes, lizards or other predatory animals.

NEVER allow your pet into your bed, you may suffocate it.

NEVER let little children play with your pet unsupervised. It is not a toy.

NEVER, when your pet is playing outside its cage, dash about with heavy footwear. Always be conscious and aware, so walk around light-footed in slippers. Remember, an adult chinchilla weighs only 18-30 ounces.

NEVER, NEVER keep your chinchilla in a one-storey cage/house.

NEVER, NEVER keep your pet permanently caged with no external exercise whatsoever. This animal is a vibrant one and will excel with plenty of exercise.

NEVER go on holiday and leave your pet to fend for itself. Always delegate a responsible person(s), preferably someone who knows your pet(s), to look after it in your absence.

NEVER allow your pet to remain sick; see a vet. Medical neglect is cruel.

NEVER sell baby chinchillas/adults without home checking. There are, unfortunately, fur farming breeders.

NEVER, if you have a breeding pair of chinchillas, continue having kittens if you have difficulty in homing the babies. DO consider having the male castrated.

NEVER let the cage/housing become dirty because you have neglected to clean it out each week, with a major clean once a month.

NEVER let your pet be without food, water, salt block and gnawing stone (pumice).

The Chinchilla
A warm ball of silk marshmallow enclosed in your hands, a delight.
It's your pet you hold gently, your friend, a furry mite.
The pleasure it gives is unsurpassed, it trusts you, it relies on you.
In return you must look after it, give it a most euphoric life too.

BIBLIOGRAPHY

Bickel, Edmund **Chinchilla Handbook** TFH (1987)
Harris, Jack **A Complete Introduction** TFH (1987)
Coulton, Jean C **Practical Chinchilla Keeping** Nimrod Press Ltd (1989)
Zeinert, Karen **All About Chinchillas** TFH (1986)
Kuhner, Horst **Step by Step Book About Chinchillas** TFH (1988)
Roderthiede, Maike **Chinchillas** Barron's Educational Series (1993)

Chinchilla Chat Line: 01752 256053
(run by author Roger Whear)